# Diagonal Man
## Theory & Praxis

### Volume I

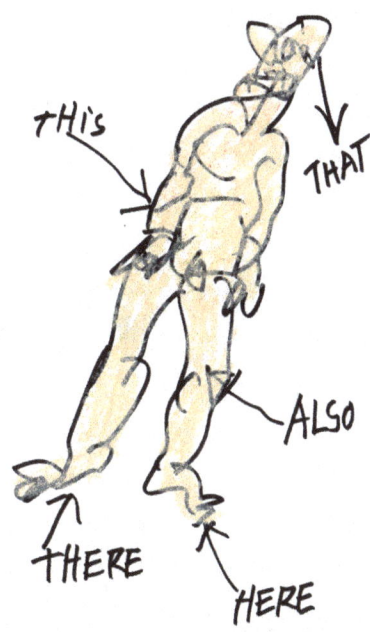

**Peter Schumann**
**Bread & Puppet**

Copyright © 2019 by Peter Schumann

All rights reserved. No part of this book may be reproduced in any form or by any means without the prior written consent, except in the case of brief quotations used in reviews and certain other noncommercial uses permitted by copyright law.

ISBN-13: 978-1-947917-05-7
Fomite
58 Peru Street
Burlington, VT 05401

<u>WHAT</u>

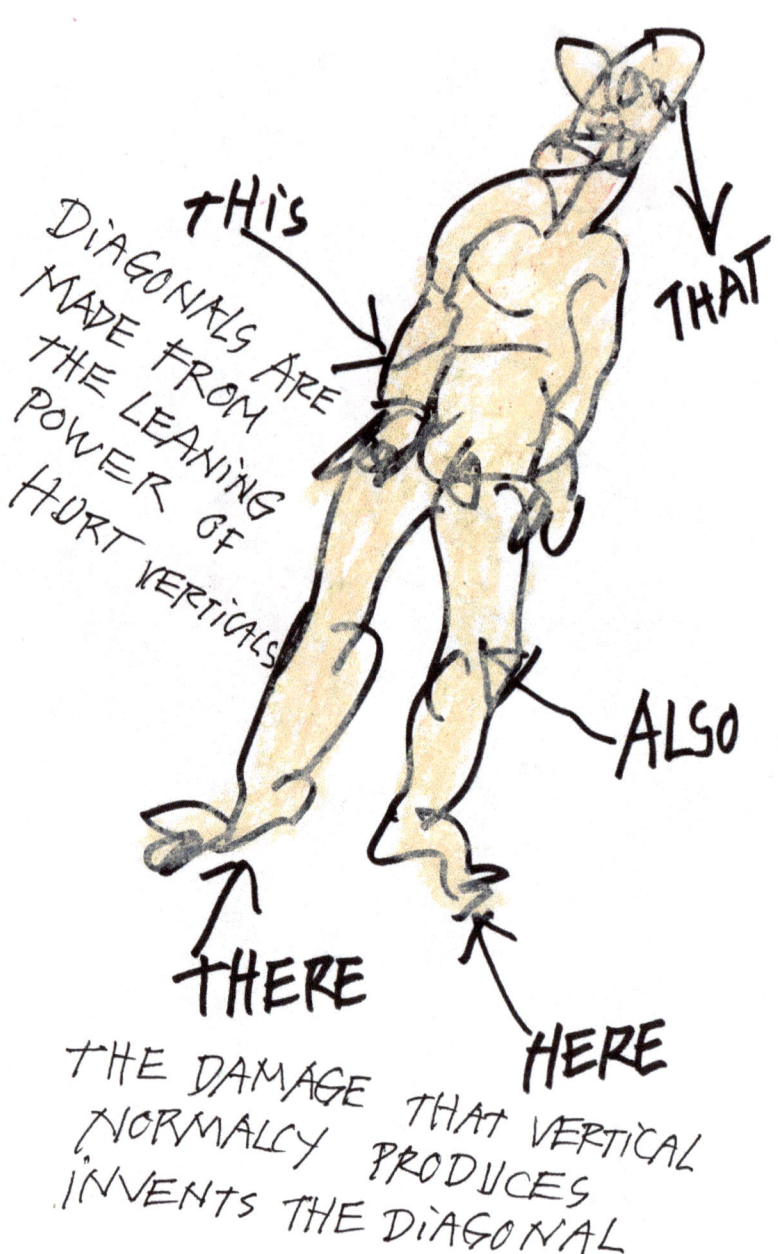

# AND PRAXIS

# THE DIAGONAL

means:
   a) IMMINENT DANGER
   b) THE NEED FOR SPLIT-SECOND ACTION TO TOSS THE DISASTER-INCLINED BODY AWAY FROM DISASTER

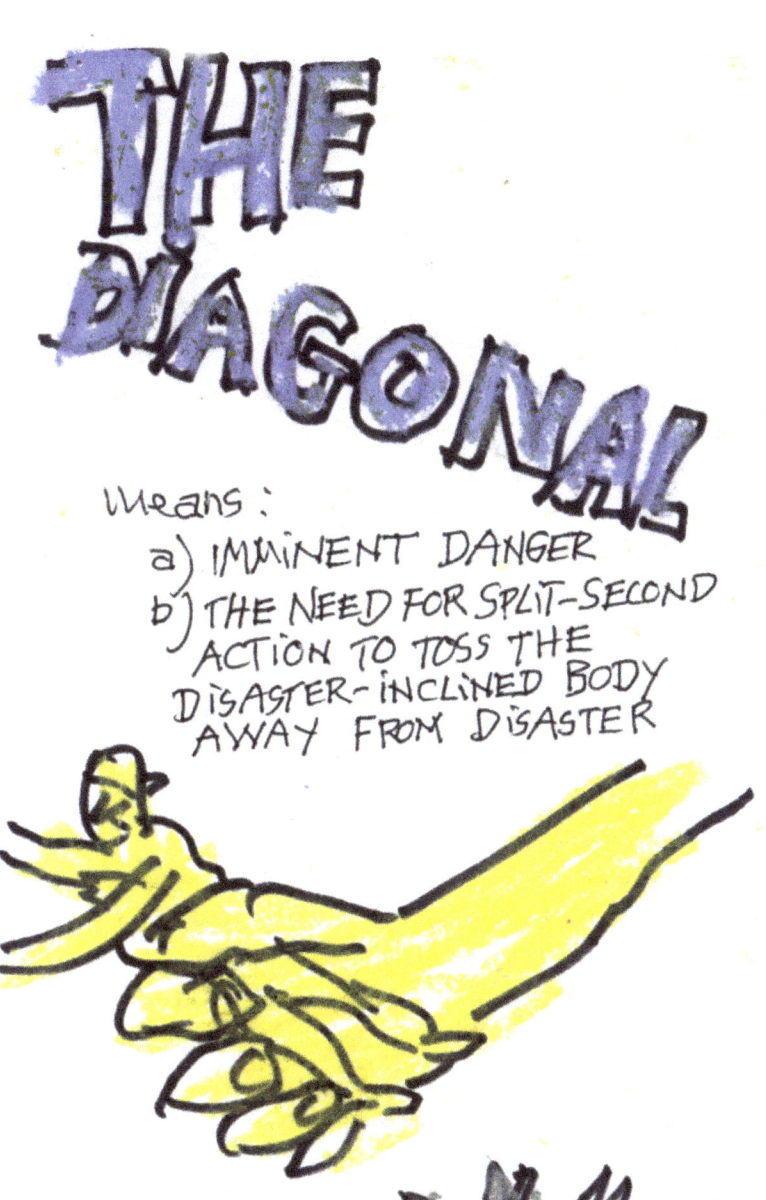

# THE PLANET

IS INHABITED BY POPULATIONS WHO ARE RAISED DIAGONALLY BY A DIAGONAL ECONOMY THAT SERVES THE DISTORTED LUXURY FEW. HISTORY HAS FORCED THIS DISPROPORTION INTO SEEMINGLY UNSHAKEABLE PERMANENCE

# THE SUN

is an effort of humangous proportion to warm humanity's shadowed underside

THE SUN SAYS:

SAVIOR CONDITIONS AS CREATED BY ANTI-PLANETARY BEHAVIOR ARE IN NEED OF IMMINENT SAVIOR PROPOSALS

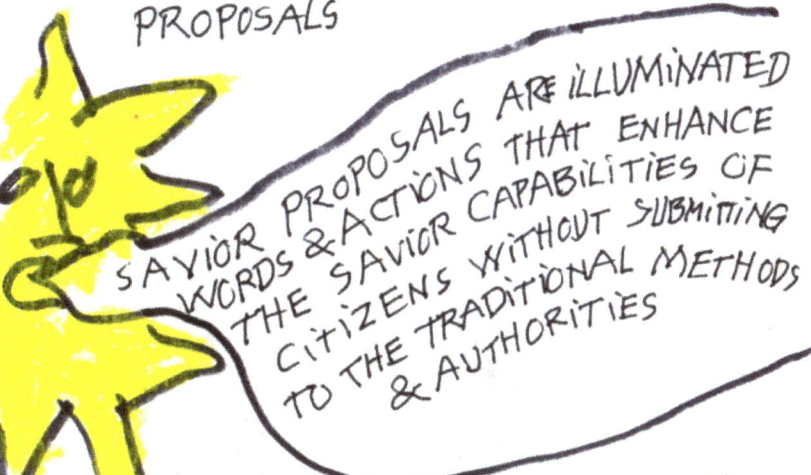

SAVIOR PROPOSALS ARE ILLUMINATED WORDS & ACTIONS THAT ENHANCE THE SAVIOR CAPABILITIES OF CITIZENS WITHOUT SUBMITTING TO THE TRADITIONAL METHODS & AUTHORITIES

# AND NOW

GIANT POSSIBILITARIAN SUNS ARE REQUIRED TO BE PARADED THROUGH THE DIAGONAL SHADOWS OF THE INTOLERABLE FALLING POSITION & TRAIN THE SUFFERERS' LIFTING MUSCLES & ENLIGHTEN HUMANITY'S LIFTING POWER

 THEREFORE THE PROPOSALS PROPOSE:

 THE DEFIANT ANTI-WARRIOR & NON-FIGHTING ACROBAT PACKED WITH THE EXTRAORDINARY MUSCLES OF LEISURE & INACTIVITY, A NON-DOING PHILOSOPHER WHOSE CONTEMPLATIONS DEPRIVE EVERY-DAY FRENZY OF ITS SUCCESS. A NON-ACTIVIST WHOSE PASSIVITY REMEDIES STRESSED-OUT LIMBS & THOUGHTS & RELIEVES ACHES BY SUBTRACTING TIME & ITS MERCHANDISE

 THE DIAGONAL ARCHITECT WHO BUILDS WALLS WHICH CRUMBLE AS THEY ARE ERECTED

C THE MIRACLE WORKER WHO — LIKE ANY MESSIAH — PUTS TINY SEEDS INTO THE FRESHLY DUG GROUND & THEN WATCHES & POINTS OUT THE MIRACLE OF THEIR GROWTH INTO LUXURIOUS GREENS

**D** COUNTER-CULTURE PROVOCATEUR RE-DIRECTS HUMANITY'S DIRECTION BY OPENING THE WINDOW & THEREBY EXPANDING THE SKY'S INTIMATE FRAGMENT TO ITS TRUE UNLIMITED MEANING & SIZE, FIT TO GUIDE ALL HUMAN HABITS & ACTIONS

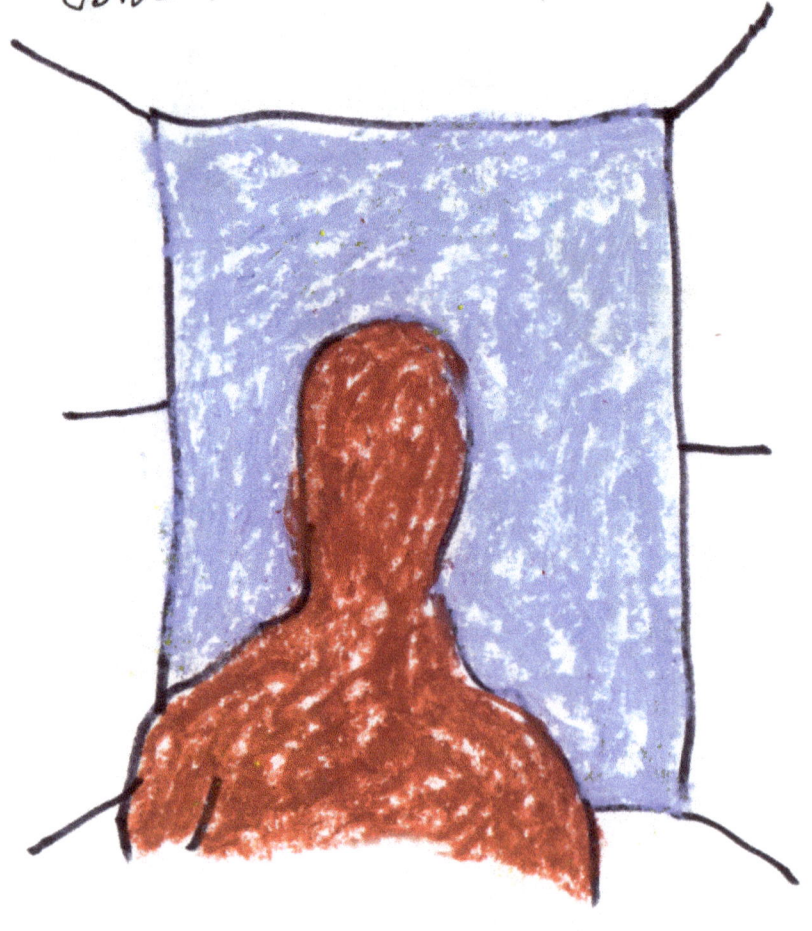

**E** GARBOLOGIST DISCOVERS THE HIDDEN MAGNIFICENCE IN ORDINARY HOUSEHOLD TRASH & WITH THE HELP OF TRASH DESIGNS BRAND NEW DIVINITIES READY FOR PUBLIC SERVICE

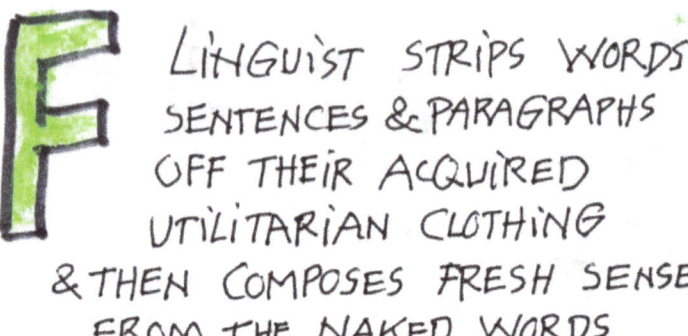

F Linguist strips words sentences & paragraphs off their acquired utilitarian clothing & then composes fresh sense from the naked words

FREE

**G** THE ROYAL EFFORT OF THE FALLING PROLETARIAT RECOGNIZED BY INSTANTANEOUS CORONATION CEREMONY AT THE PRECISE MOMENT OF NOT FALLING

**H** UNFETTERED MONEY LIBERALIST SUCCESSFULLY CONFRONTED BY SERIOUSLY EGALITARIAN SCISSORS

# I

TOTALLY FINE
DEPRIVATION APPRECIATION
SPECIALIST

 CO-DETERMINATION TECHNIQUE APPLIED TO THE SHORTLY-BEFORE-COLLAPSE SITUATION

**K** SNOW EQUALITY MEASUREMENT & ANALYSIS NOW AVAILABLE FOR ALL EGALITARIAN PURSUITS

THE NOT YET UP & ALMOST DOWN OF THE DIAGONAL IS AN INSPIRED POSITION OF LIFE. THE DIAGONALIST IS FIXED INTO THE UNFORGIVING SPACE OF THE IN-BETWEEN & THEREFORE PREDESTINED TO STRUGGLE HIS WAY OUT OF THE PREDICAMENT

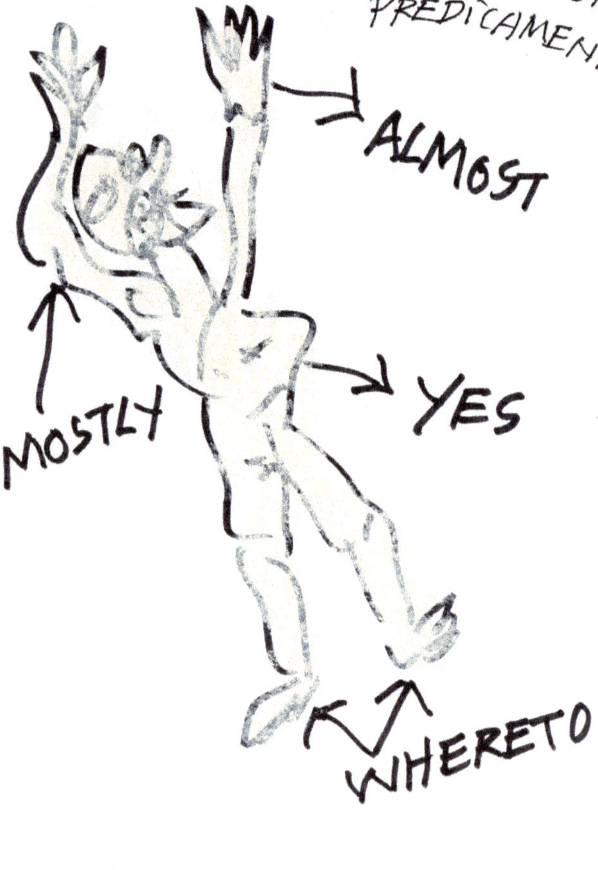

ALMOST

MOSTLY

YES

WHERETO

YOU, THE NOTHING BY YOUR SIDE, IN THE PRESENCE OF WIND, DROUGHT & RAIN! YOU, OVERUNDERMAN & SEER OF LIMITED VISION!

YOU SAY YOUR RANDOM IMPERATIVE: THOU MUST!

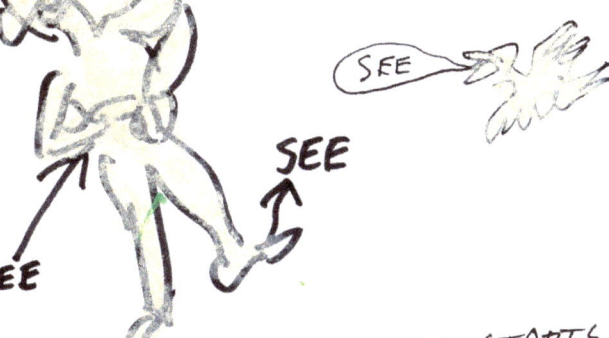

AND THUS THE WORLD STARTS ALL OVER AGAIN, ACCORDING TO THE MARCHING ORDER OF THE BELOW!

# DIAGONAL DANCING

THE GOING & LEAVING OF THE ORDINARY KIND RESULT FROM SPECIFIC TALENTS OF OUR FOREVER DANCING MUSCLES. ESSENTIALLY OUR MUSCLES NEVER SUBMIT TO THE PRAGMATIC DEMANDS OF UTILITARIAN LIFE & PRACTICE THEIR OWN JOYS & PAIN EVASIONS. THEY ARE DANCERS WHO GET THEIR TRAINING FROM THE SUPERFLUOUS MINUTES & SECONDS WHICH EVERYDAY ALLOWS FOR. THESE SELF-CONSCIOUS HOLY MINUTES REPRESENT THE HIGHEST DEGREE OF MUSCLE CREATIVITY & HELP THE DAY ACHIEVE ITS GOAL.

IF THESE DANCES DON'T ACHIEVE THEIR DIAGONAL GOAL, THEY HAVE TO BE SUPPLEMENTED WITH CARDBOARD DANCES, WHICH MEANS PAINTING & CUTTING OUT & THEN MANIPULATING THE DANCERS. THESE MANIPULATIONS ARE MEANINGFUL BECAUSE THEY RESEMBLE THE MANIPULATIONS OF THE CITIZENRY BY THE HANDS OF POLITICS & MEDIA & MUST THEREFORE BE CHOREOGRAPHED TO CLARIFY BOTH REASON & EFFECT OF THE MANIPULATION.

## From the Diagonal Perspective 1

At the boxstores where they sell men: short, tall, with or without gallbladder, mostly the habitual designer merchandise, the miraculously vertical activist, peace-loving warmonger, equipped with all necessary brutality muscles, square & gorgeous, with a self-confidence that says: humanity has already been invented, there is nothing more to do than to enforce it! Get the police enforcers who know how to do the job. Your merchandise will be delivered to your doorsteps. Its labor potential & demolition capacity are all yours, it specializes in success, which you, the owner, harvests.

## FROM THE DIAGONAL PERSPECTIVE 2

THE PRODUCTION OF DIFFICULTIES STARTS IN KINDERGARTEN & EXTENDS THROUGH ACTIVE LIFE TO THE HOSPICE SERVICES OF THE EMPIRE. DIFFICULTIES ARE NOT NAIVE: THEY NEED INVENTING, TENDING & NURSING. MODERNISTS' BRAINS, STUFFED WITH THE MYTHS OF MANY TIMES ADHERE TO THE TRADITION OF CYCLIC PROBLEM CREATION & SOLUTION, BOTH SACRED & PROFANE. UNSUBSTANTIVE CARDBOARDMAN AS CREATED BY MAN IS AS DISPENSABLE AS MAN & AS PREDESTINED BY HIS MYTHOLOGY, HIS SHORT EXISTENCE BEFORE IMMOLATION A SPECTACLE TO BEHOLD

## FROM THE DIAGONAL PERSPECTIVE 3

ON HIS WAY TO THE BATTLEFIELD DIAGONAL MAN MEETS THE DWARVES, ALL JOLLY & ROSY-CHEEKED, CLIMBING ROSY-CHEEKED APPLETREES AT THE EDGE OF THE ABYSS, LOUDLY PROCLAIMING THEIR LUST FOR APPLES AS THEY SPREAD THROUGHOUT THE BRANCHES BLASTING TRUMPETS & FLUGELHORNS LIKE THE ROYAL BRASS ENSEMBLES OF OLD.

THE DWARVES' PHILOSOPHY IS APPARENT IN THEIR BEHAVIOR — THEY PRACTICE BROTHERLY & SISTERLY LOVE AS THEY FILL THEIR BASKETS WITH ROSY-CHEEKED APPLES, HALTING ONLY OCCASIONALLY WHEN A WORM IS DETECTED & DILIGENTLY REMOVED.

DWARVES ORIGINATE IN COMMUNITIES THAT PRACTICE CONSEQUENTIAL THINKING & THEN ACQUIRE AN ADEQUATELY SMALL LIFESTYLE IN OPPOSITION TO THE FASHIONABLE COMMON LIFESTYLE OF GIGANTISM.

## DIAGONAL MAN'S COMET OBSERVATORY

How can the comet get here if we are so overly concerned with our unconvincing selves' well-being? How can the comet achieve its high-falutin' goals with our state-of-mind so alien to its arrival? Our only constancy is in our indulgence in government-produced facts, not in our birth-right expectations that we deserve. We only dream the sky, we don't see it. We want, but insufficiently so. Wants, which are indiscriminate, actually want us, but our responses are too dull for them

# THE PHALANSTERY

THE DIAGONAL PHALANSTERY IS MOSTLY ATTENDED BY GRADUATES OF THE WORKFORCE WHO ARE IN THE PROCESS OF UNLEARNING THE WASTEFUL TIME & BRAIN DRAINING HABITS OF THAT INSTITUTION & CONSEQUENTLY ARE COMMITTED TO BEING DWARVES IN THE FACE OF THE POPULAR GIGANTISM SYSTEM

THE PHALANSTERY IS MEANT FOR REHABILITATION OF VERTICAL NORMALCY & NEEDS TO TRAIN THE BRAIN FOR THE WORLDVIEW OF THE IN-BETWEEN WHICH IS AN OPPRESSED & OFTEN ILLEGAL WORLDVIEW OPPOSITE THE WELL-EDUCATED SCHIZOPHRENIA OF THE ACCEPTED WORLDVIEW.

THE DIAGONAL PHALANSTERY OFFERS LESSONS IN INTERIOR NAVIGATION THAT ENABLE THE STUDENTS TO TRAVERSE THE MIGHTY LAND INSIDE THE DIAGONAL BODY & FOLLOW THEIR ARTERIES' HUDSON OR CONNECTICUT RIVERS INTO THE PORTS TO WHICH THE FRUITS & FOODS GET DELIVERED.

THAT MICROCOSM'S MIGHTY LAND IS BRIMMING OVER WITH CITIES OF BUGS & MICROBES, BACTERIA & PARASITES & SPARKLING WITH JUNGLES FULL OF TIGERS & SNAKES, DESERTS WITH CAMELS & VULTURES, STEPPES WITH ZEBRAS & ELEPHANTS, ALL PART OF THE EARTH WITHIN THE EARTH INSIDE THE DIAGONAL BODY, WHICH IS AN IN-BETWEEN & UNDECIDED BODY THAT ABSORBS THE STARS OF THE HEAVEN ABOVE & DISTRIBUTES ITS LIGHT EFFECTIVELY INTO ITS OWN DARKNESS.

AND THEN THE MOUTH OF THE DIAGONAL BODY OPENS & ADDRESSES THE TYPIFYERS & REPRESENTATIVES OF THE MODERN WORLD: YOU ARE NOT CARDBOARD YET & LACK THE GOING-AWAY GRACE OF THE 2-DIMENSIONAL HEROIC WORLD, BUT YOU MUST REALIZE THE PLANETARY FUNCTIONS & BATTLES IN YOUR VERY OWN FLESH-BODIES WHICH YOUR MOTHERS GAVE TO YOU AFTER RECEIVING THEM FROM THEIR VERY OWN MOTHER EARTH!

YOU MUST ALLOW YOUR EYES TO PENETRATE THE BENEVOLENT ~~FOG~~ WHICH YOUR OWN PRETENTIOUS HISTORY HAS EXHALED & SPREAD WIDELY OVER YOUR PRODUCTION: YOUR ISOLATION EMPIRE WHICH SEPERATES YOU FROM THE DEMOCRACY INSIDE YOU: THE LANDSCAPES OF BUGS & BACTERIA THAT RULE YOUR UNKNOWN TERRITORY & WANT TO SETTLE YOUR WASTELAND WITH BILLIONS OF STARS THAT LIE IN WAITING FOR YOU!

# AND THEN

THE DIAGONAL PREACHER CLIMBED UP A VERY TALL LADDER & FROM THE TOP OF THE LADDER HE POINTED TO THE YELLOW CLOUDS ABOVE & HE SAID:
TAKE NOTICE OF THIS INCOMPARABLE YELLOW THAT THE SKY HAS IN STORE FOR YOU!

# BEWARE

OF THE SHALLOW LIFE THAT NEGLECTS THE SKY'S YELLOW!
**Brighten** THE DARK FACTS WITH THAT YELLOW! THE FACTS THEMSELVES MUST BE ALTERED TO FIT THAT YELLOW LIGHT & DESTROY THE ARROGANT DETAILS WHICH RULE THE DARKNESS & ORGANIZE ITS UNNECESSARY PAIN!

## EQUIP YOURSELF

WITH A YELLOW EDUCATION!
A BRAND-NEW ONE OUTSIDE THE
EDUCATIONAL SYSTEM! ONE THAT IS
INFORMED BY THE SKY'S YELLOW!
ONE THAT COLLABORATES WITH THE
HUDSON RIVER IN YOUR ARTERIES!
ONE THAT INSISTS ON THE DIAGONAL
DISTORTION OF THE SICKLY VERTICAL
STRIFE!

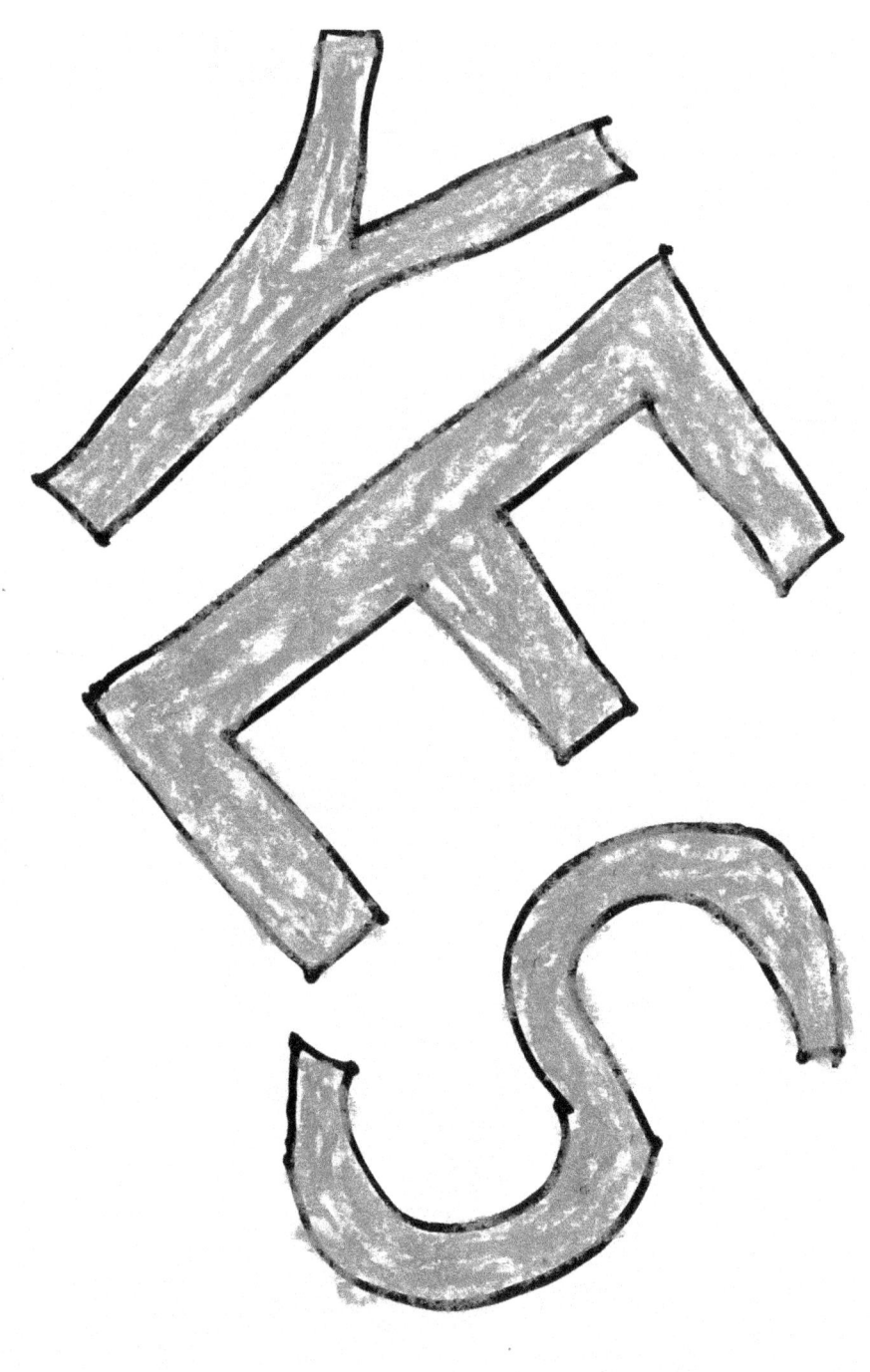

BREATHE THE CLOUDS & THE THUNDER STORMS! BREATHE THE HERONS & THE GEESE! BREATHE THE CRICKETS & THE FIREBUGS INTO YOUR LUNGS! FOLLOW THE INSURRECTION OF YOUR UNDISCOVERED MIND!

IMPOSE YOUR VISION ON THE HIGHWAY SYSTEM THAT PRETENDS TO TAKE YOU TO YOUR DESIDERATUM BUT INSTEAD TIES YOU TO A SEAT THAT ASPIRES TO BE YOUR BOSS! ADDRESS THE HIGHWAY! TELL IT TO CARRY YOU INTO YOUR OWN VEINS WHICH WILL TRANSPORT YOU TO YOUR OWN HEART & TO YOUR OWN HEART'S DESIRE! TO ACHIEVE THE EDEN THAT HAS NOT BEEN INVENTED YET!

**THE** MANY OBVIOUS DARKNESSES ALL AROUND US ALL AGREE:
**DAWN** HAS TO BE ACHIEVED!
**THE** HORIZON MUST BE HELPED!
**TO** PRODUCE THE SUNRISE!

CHORUSSES HAVE TO BE REHEARSED, LINE-DANCERS CHOREOGRAPHED! ALL MANNER OF OVERSIZED GODS HAVE TO BE MADE FROM PAPERMACHÉ & MANIPULATED INTO PROPER POSITION TO ASSURE THE FESTIVE EXTRAVAGANCE OWED TO THE SUNRISE! **ONLY** SUNRISES CAN SAVE US FROM OURSELVES! & CORRECT OUR OTHERWISE UNCORRECTED MANNER OF LIFE, BECAUSE OUR TRADITIONAL CORRECTIONAL FACILITIES HAVE FAILED US SO BADLY!

A VAST ARRAY OF REPRESENTATIVES OF THE ANIMAL KINGDOM: COCKROACHES & LIONS, BUTTERFLIES & GIRAFFES, SNAILS & FROGS, PONIES & SLUGS, SHARKS & CRANES, DRAGONS & CRICKETS ALL CONTRIBUTE TO POMP & CIRCUMSTANCE & NEED TO BE HOSTED IN A DIGNIFIED MANNER. THE TASK IS ENORMOUS! THE FEAST MUST BE CORRECT & CANNOT AFFORD ANY MISTAKE IN DETAIL & EXECUTION OF CEREMONY!

**ALL WIDELY ACCEPTED ASSUMPTIONS OF ORDINARY PERCEPTION CONCERNING THE LIGHT OF DAY MUST YIELD TO THIS SINGULAR SERMON OF MAGNIFICENCE**

**ALL** population segments whether dwarfish or gigantic, deprived or spoiled, fat or 2-dimensional must attend. Nobody will be excused. **BECAUSE** the door to the sunrise must be opened communally all-embracingly. Only then can the sun rise effectively in accordance with its mission & meaning

# AND THEN

THE DIAGONAL PREACHER DESCENDED FROM HIS TALL LADDER & JOINED THE CARDBOARD MASSES THAT ROAMED THROUGH THE OUTSKIRTS OF THE CITY & THEN POURED DOWN THE INTERSTATE IN THE DIRECTION OF THE YELLOW LIGHT

# AND THUS

THE FLESH RE-AFFIRMS ITSELF & THE MUSCLES REGAIN THEIR TRANSFORMATIVE STRENGTH TO GUIDE THE MIND'S TOUCHING POWER & HELP REORGANIZE THE SHALLOW ½ WORLD AGAINST ITS ESTABLISHED TRAFFIC & GIVE IT THE BLOSSOMING DIRECTION OF ITS OWN INSIDE

# AND THUS

THE HALF-HEARTED WILL ARISE! TO BE WHOLE-HEARTED!

# AND

THE DROWSY EMPIRE CITIZEN WILL AWAKEN

# AND

DEMAND THE FULL GLORY THAT THE EMPIRE'S HALF-MIND CANNOT DELIVER

# THE WAR ISSUE

WITH QUOTES FROM
BIBLE & ISAAC BABEL

# THEY DO

THEY GO ON & ON WITH HARDLY A BREATHING STOP, PANTING LIKE EXHAUSTED DOGS, LEANING FORWARD, GETTING THERE OR NOT, SWEATING, MOANING & GROANING TOWARDS THE INDEFINITE FORWARD WITH ITS MIRIAD DEMANDS.

# THEY HEAR

THE EMERGENCY SIRENS RINGING IN THEIR EARS LONG AFTER THEY HAVE FADED INTO THE DISTANCE.

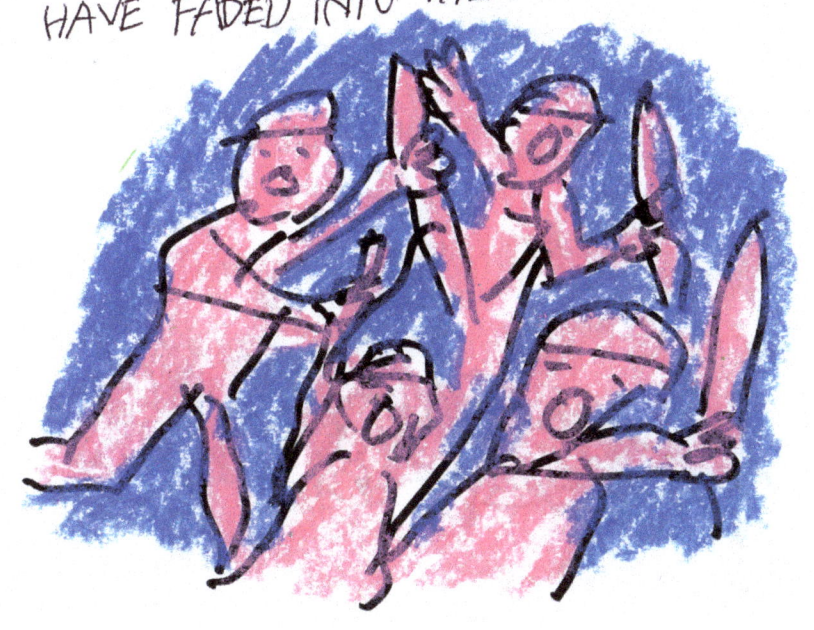

THE GOD OF HURRY WHIPS THEM ALONG. WILD-EYED BEASTS STARE AT THEM. BIRDS FLEE FROM THEM. INSECTS WITHDRAW FROM THEIR PATH.

SINGLE-MINDED RETAINERS & STOPPERS, THINKERS & SEERS CAN'T STOP THEM & EVEN AS THEY SICKEN & COLLAPSE FROM THEIR ENORMOUS OVERWORK THEY CANNOT BE HELD BACK. THE AIR THEY SUCK INTO THEIR LUNGS ORDERS THEM FORWARD

ON+ON +ON +ON+ON +ON +ON+ON
+ON +ON +ON +ON +ON +ON +ON
+ON+ON +ON+ON +ON+ ON +ON+ON
+ON +ON +ON +ON +ON +ON+ON
+ON +ON +ON +ON +ON +ON+ON
+ON+ON+ON +ON +ON +ON+ON
+ON+ON+ON +ON +ON +ON+ON
+ON +ON +ON +ON +ON +ON +ON
+ON +ON +ON +ON +ON +ON+ON
+ON +ON +ON+ON +ON +ON+ON
+ON +ON +ON +ON +ON +ON
+ON +ON +ON +ON +ON +ON
+ON +ON +ON +ON +ON +ON
+ON +ON +ON +ON+ON +ON
+ON +ON +ON +ON +ON +ON
+ON + ON +ON +ON +ON +ON
+ON +ON +ON +ON +ON +ON
+ON +ON+ON +ON +ON+ON

**THE** BOSS SAID TO THE GENERAL: LOOK I HAVE DELIVERED THE CITY INTO YOUR HANDS. YOU SHALL MARCH AROUND THE CITY WITH ALL YOUR FIGHTING MEN, MAKING THE CIRCUIT OF IT ONCE, FOR 6 DAYS RUNNING & 7 PRIESTS WITH 7 TRUMPETS MADE FROM RAMS' HORNS. ON THE 7th DAY YOU SHALL MARCH ROUND THE CITY 7 TIMES & THE PRIESTS SHALL BLOW THEIR TRUMPETS. AT THE BLAST OF THE RAMS' HORNS THE WHOLE ARMY SHALL RAISE A GREAT SHOUT & THE WALL OF THE CITY WILL COLLAPSE & THE ARMY SHALL ADVANCE. THE CITY SHALL BE UNDER SOLEMN BAN: EVERYTHING IN IT BELONGS TO THE BOSS. NO ONE IS TO BE SPARED. ALL THE SILVER & GOLD SHALL BE HOLY THEY BELONG TO THE BOSS & MUST GO INTO HIS TREASURY. THEN THEY DESTROYED EVERYTHING IN THE CITY, THEY PUT EVERYONE TO THE SWORD, MEN & WOMEN, YOUNG & OLD, ALSO CATTLE, SHEEP & ASSES.

THE COLORFUL SQUADRON CAME RIDING UP THE HIGHROAD, THEIR EMACIATED BUT SPIRITED HORSES TROTTING AT A STEADY PACE IN FIERY PILLARS OF DUST. MAGNIFICENT BANNERS WERE FLUTTERING ON GUILDED POLES WEIGHED DOWN BY VELVET TASSELS. THE HORSEMEN RODE WITH MAJESTIC & INSOLENT HAUGHTINESS. THE TATTERED FOOTSOLDIERS CAME CRAWLING OUT OF THEIR TRENCHES & WITH THEIR MOUTHS HANGING OPEN WATCHED THE LIGHTFOOTED ELEGANCE OF THE UNRUFFLED STREAM.

# HOW

TO EFFECTIVELY MAKE THE NON-WAR CULTURE BECOME USEFUL TO THE DOMINANT CULTURE WHICH IS THE PERMANENT WAR CULTURE & REDIRECT HUMAN PRODUCTION TO SERVE ITS NEEDS

# HOW

TO TURN NOT ONLY THE PLANET'S RAW MATERIALS BUT ALSO HUMAN FLESH & THOUGHT INTO ESSENTIAL RESOURCES FOR PERMANENT WAR

# AHAHOH

# DARK

CLOUDS CONCENTRATE THE ALREADY OUTRAGED SKY & SUBJUGATE THE LANDSCAPE TO THE GATHERING INSIDE IT

A) ASSEMBLING THE BATTLEGEAR
B) THE CONVENTION OF THE WARRIORS
C) THE DRILLING OF THE BATTLE STEEDS
D) THE BOOTCAMP FOR THE AS YET UNINITIATED CITIZENS WHO MUST BE FITTED FOR THE REQUIRED TASK: TO BE SUITED FOR ALL APPROPRIATE ATROCITIES IN 5 OR 6 STEPS.

STEP 1: REDESIGN HEADS FOR SOLDIERING.

STEP 2: COLLECT ALL AVAILABLE JUNK, CARDBOARD BOXES, FABRIC SCRAPS, ALL MANNER OF STICKS

STEP 3: PICKUP TRUCK FILLED WITH SAP BUCKETS TRAVELS TO RIVERBANK TO GET CLAY

STEP 4: CLAY GETS DUMPED INTO DISCARDED BATHTUBS + WATER ADDED

STEP 5: STOMPING FEET KNEAD CLAY TO THE TUNE OF COMMON BATTLE HYMNS

STEP 6: HANDS MIX HAY INTO CLAY

# THEN

HANDS SET OUT TO MOLD THE FINAL MODEL OF THE TOTALLY EXACT FUTURE SOLDIER, THE CLASSICAL OBEDIENT DESTRUCTION EXPERT, THE DREAM OF ALL GENERALS, FITTED TO EXECUTE ANY FEROCIOUS STRATEGY FOR THE WHERE EVER, WHEN EVER, WHOSO EVER.

# THE

1. BATALLION SPECIALIZES IN EXTRA SMALL ENEMIES THEREFORE ATTACKS WITH MOSQUITOS

# THE

2. BATALLION EMPLOYS TANKS BUILT FROM BULLSHIT (TARGETS MEDIUM SIZE ENEMIES)

**THE** 3RD BATALLION THE ONE THAT HAS NOT BEEN DEFEATED YET, CITIES UNDER THEIR HOOVES, COMETS IN THEIR HAIR, RIVERS & MOUNTAINS IN THEIR COMPANIONSHIP. FLOCKS OF STARLINGS & GEESE ABOVE. CLOUDS BUILD IMPENETRABLE WALLS AS LIGHTRAYS ISSUE FROM THE ABOVE & JUBILEER CHORUSSES RUN TOWARD THEIR TRAIL TO JOIN THEM. TREES BEND TO LET THEM PASS. THE WHOLE McDONALD'S CIVILIZATION FALLS TO ITS KNEES TO ALLOW THEIR VICTORY

# WHEN

THEY ARE NOT HORSES THEY FALTER
OR PIOUSLY GO ALONG

# WHEN

THEY ARE THEY DON'T MIND FROST
& WIND & BEAR WITNESS TO UNBORN SUCCESS

HORSE HIGH ABOVE THE CITY INTERFERING WITH HORIZONTAL TRAFFIC-AS-USUAL, DESTABILIZING CONFORMED REALITY

# HORSE = REALITY's
## Submission to Diagonal Subjectmatter

# OUR HORSES

DEFINE OUR STRENGTH & NEIGHING:
JUBILATION + GRATITUDE

# AND

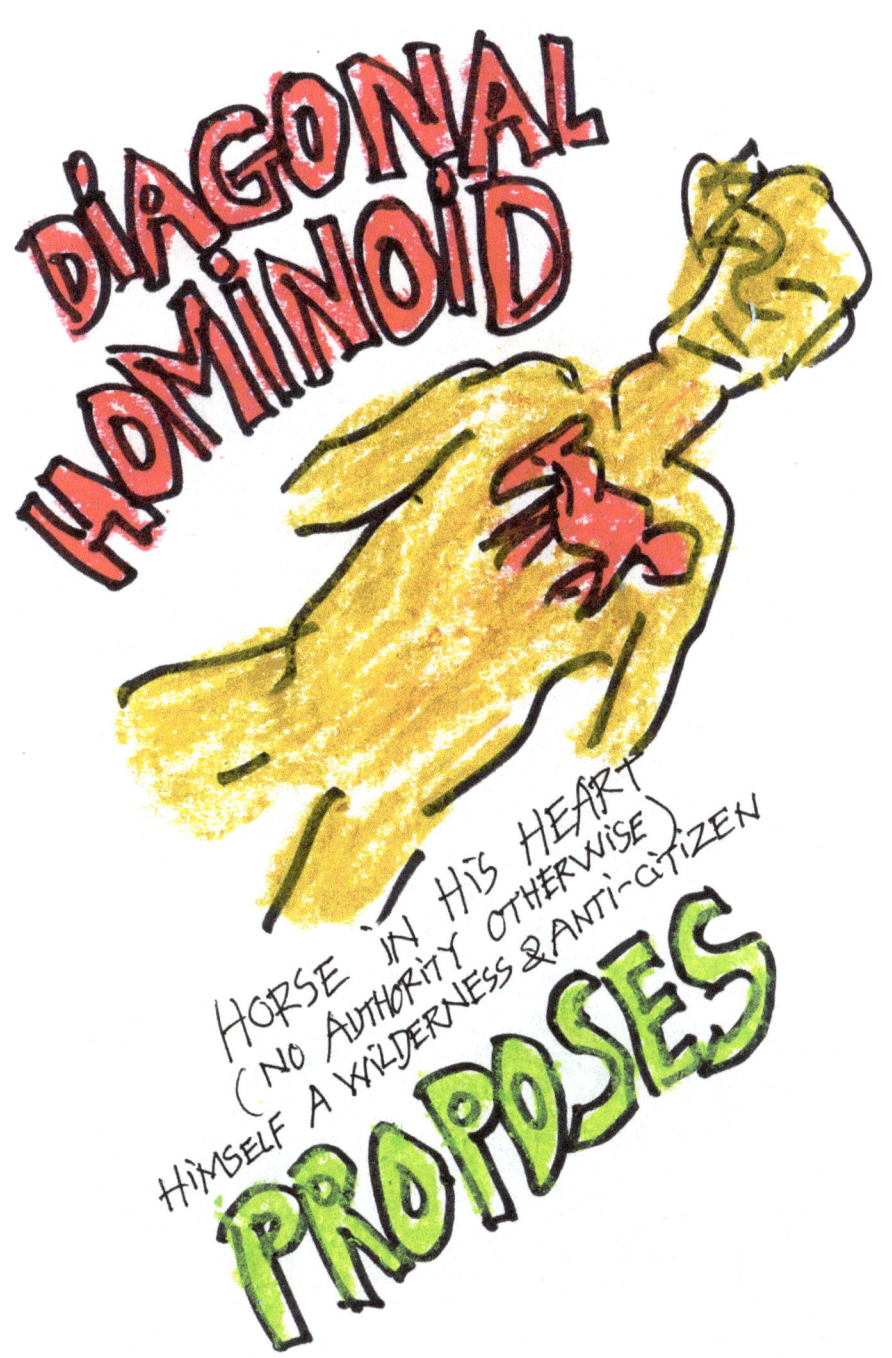

# DIAGONAL STAMPEDE IN GREAT MEADOW